28 DAY JO

7
RULES
TO A
GOOD
LIFE

SELF-DEVELOPMENT PROGRAMME
(with a little help from me)

DAVE ARMSTRONG

An audio-visual package supports this Journal available on: Live Life Smarter YouTube Channel (subscription required) https://www.youtube.com/@ livelifesmartercoachingpro6615/featured

ISBN: 978-1-7385381-9-5

Special acknowledgement to C J Harter www.cjharterbooks.co.uk for the support in getting the book from idea-stage to the page.

Cover and interior design by Victoria Wolf, wolfdesignandmarketing.com

Hardback and paperback editions of this Journal are available.

In support of this Journal there is a 1 hr 30 min Personal Development Planning Session available on the website: 7rules2agoodlife.com

This Journal is supported by the book 7 Rules to a Good Life available on Audible, Paperback, Hardback and E-book. Audible version recorded by Greg Veryard at 80Hrz Studio. Audible narrated by Jed Simpson.

THIS 28-DAY JOURNAL IS CREATED BY DAVE ARMSTRONG AND DRIVEN BY YOU.

THE CHALLENGES YOU ARE ABOUT to set yourself are uniquely yours. So, don't have doubt or be fearful: YOU can achieve whatever you believe in or want to do, and YOU can become the person you want to be. All it takes is a dollop of desire, iron determination, hard work (both physically and mentally), and a dose of persistence. More importantly, make sure it is done with a smile inside.

You are and will be the person YOU think you are. So, celebrate being YOU, like being YOU and love being YOU. Whether you are struggling in the lows of life or achieving peak performance, this 28-day self-coaching programme will apply to YOU.

This self-coaching programme is yours, so choose your challenges wisely.

Remember: life is not a quick fix, but it is the daily compounding of good habits that leads to excellent behaviours. Over the forthcoming 28 days you will have ups and downs. But don't get too carried away with success and don't get down when things don't go so well. Just pick yourself up, dust yourself off each day and 'GO AGAIN'.

 If you really want the good life you desire, remember this mantra: 'do something today to make you better (and happier) tomorrow'. Following this advice, you will not go far wrong.

Good luck. I believe in you; more importantly, believe in yourself.

CONTENTS

WELCOME TO YOUR
7 RULES TO A GOOD LIFE
28-DAY JOURNAL

THERE ARE TWO CERTAINTIES IN LIFE: you are born, and you die. The uncertainty is found in the bit between. The unknown in life is when it will end. If we are honest with ourselves, we all want to live a good life. The good news is the good life is here, if you want it.

This personal daily *7 Rules* 28-day Journal will help you achieve the good life you desire.

Everything you need for a positive life is inside your mind. This Journal will help you bring it out, so you can get as much out of your life as possible in a safe and constructive way. This Journal will create a learning environment for you to master success in everything you do, in whatever life you wish to lead.

The fact is that what you think you are, you will be. The brain is the greatest computer, but it is driven and developed through our experiences, thoughts and emotions which ultimately form our habits, attitudes and behaviours, and are created by the decisions we make and the actions we take (or do not take) across all parts of our lives. This learning journey starts at the moment we are born and ends only when we close our eyes for the last time.

Remember this: the agency you take each day is yours and the responsibility that goes with it is also yours; so, choose wisely. You can help yourself by ensuring the experiences you expose yourself to are good ones (receive agency), and when you do experience something, you control the battle of the mind (feel agency).

No wilful lying now. Make sure everything you do is based on truth and is set in a positive environment that leads to the beneficial outcomes necessary for growing and living your good life.

Don't be a bystander in your own life. Grab it with both hands and start living the good life now. Be 'on point' for all risk and issues within your life, and you will become your own lighthouse and maybe a lighthouse for others.

Be confident and break those chains, move into the light and become the real you, the beautiful you, the true you.

You only get one life; this Journal will help you make sure your life is a good one.

The 7 Rules to a Good Life

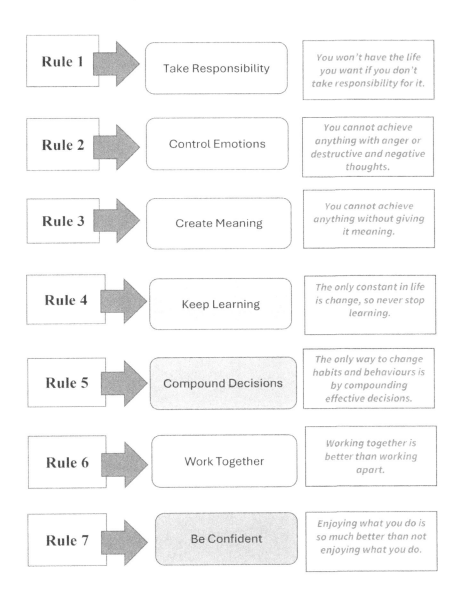

Rule 1	Take Responsibility	You won't have the life you want if you don't take responsibility for it.
Rule 2	Control Emotions	You cannot achieve anything with anger or destructive and negative thoughts.
Rule 3	Create Meaning	You cannot achieve anything without giving it meaning.
Rule 4	Keep Learning	The only constant in life is change, so never stop learning.
Rule 5	Compound Decisions	The only way to change habits and behaviours is by compounding effective decisions.
Rule 6	Work Together	Working together is better than working apart.
Rule 7	Be Confident	Enjoying what you do is so much better than not enjoying what you do.

YOUR REFLECTIVE DAILY PERSONAL DEVELOPMENT PLANNING JOURNAL

THIS *7 RULES TO A GOOD LIFE* 28-DAY JOURNAL is the place to write down your daily reflections, thoughts and feelings.

Your daily reflection should be about what you do in the day. Carrying out a self-reflection allows you to learn and grow daily from the decisions you take and experiences you have over that day.

Remember: the daily compounding of your habits forms your behaviour and attitude to life. Doing something positive today that you are proud of, or dealing with something you are not so happy with, will lead to your better tomorrow, better week, better month, better year and better life.

This Journal will help you remember and recall important learning events that have happened across your life. It will help you reflect upon what you do through the week. Actively actioning your Wheel of a

Balanced Life will lead you to a fulfilled life. Managing and actioning your Peak Performance Profile will lead you to excel in life.

Setting yourself personal weekly challenges will keep you ahead of life's curve and ensure you gain in life rather than drift.

If you work on your Journal each day, each week, each month and each year, you will gradually create your own library of references for improvement that you can call upon. More importantly, you will build and design your own personal philosophy.

As you grow over the days, weeks, months and years, you will increase your understanding of what happens in your life. You will learn to self-moderate as you go and align future decisions with your values and principles; basically, you will learn from your experiences and maintain and grow your good life.

Your reflective Journal helps you to continually do something today to make you better tomorrow.

In support of this Journal, there is a 1 hr 30 min
Personal Development Planning Session available
via the website: https://7rules2agoodlife.com

NB: by accessing the Personal Development Planning Session
you will be bringing togther all elements of the learning
process: Verbal (hearing), Visual (seeing) and Kinesthetic
(doing). You will enhance your learning experience, releas-
ing your full potential and increasing your levels of success.

HOW TO USE
THE JOURNAL

JUST WRITE IT, AND WRITE IT EVERY DAY. You will not regret it. Give yourself some time out of your day, either at the end or at the beginning of the next day, to capture what you do and how you feel about it.

Think of this: you will go to the gym or take up exercise, and you will cook healthy food, to help your body and control your weight. Helping your mind is just as important, and in fact has more value. In that time you set aside, you can reflect, moderate and 'go again' each day. The compounding effect of that daily habit will create your learning habit, set your learning behaviour and form your learning attitude; leading you to a good life.

Ideally, set aside 15 minutes of your day to write your Journal. You can do it either at the end of the day or write your entry first thing the following morning. Make sure, when you write, you are in a personal space that allows you to think, allows you to reflect on the day in a calm and relaxed manner. You deserve that time, so grab it. Once you have written your comments, put the Journal aside and 'go again'.

The habits

- Set your Wheel of a Balanced Life.
- Set your Peak Performance Profile.
- On a daily basis, reflect on your day using the *7 Rules*.
- On a weekly basis, reflect on whether you have drifted or gained in that week.
- On a weekly basis, set yourself challenges for the next week.
- Reflect on your Wheel of a Balanced Life.
- Reflect on your Peak Performance Profile.
- Across the 28 days, when you have an important experience write it down and reflect upon it, so you can recall it when needed.
- At the start of the 28 days, set yourself a personal contract. At the end of the 28 days, reflect upon that contract, modify it and then set it again.

Set your personal contract

A KEY PART OF CREATING MEANING and direction in your life is the setting of goals from the visualisations you do. The power of a personal contract is that it helps you keep your life on track with meaning. Your personal contract runs across your whole life and will grow as your skill, knowledge and experience grow. This chimes with my *7 Rules to a Good Life* and **Rule 4: Keep Learning**. If you want to achieve your personal goals and be the best you can be each day, creating a personal contract will keep you focussed on the pathway towards those goals. A personal contract is a personal commitment to yourself. It is a written one-page statement of what you want to achieve as well as how to achieve it. A personal contract is a powerful self-motivator. It motivates you to create effective habits and set personal values to keep to each day in line with your life goals. Whether that is losing weight or running your own business, the general principles of a personal contract influence every level of your life. Like everything with living a smarter life, the simpler and more achievable the personal contract is, the easier it is to honour. The foundation of the personal contract is set around the character you would like to be and the values you want to live by. The power of the personal contract is in embedding it within your soul and taking responsibility for it in its entirety. The contract you design is solely down to you to fulfil. Do not let yourself down and wonderful things will happen.

So, dream your dreams, visualise them and from them create meaning within all parts of your life. If you let your left brain meet your right brain, and you can GROW your life in a positive direction, everything is possible. Take responsibility for all you do, control the emotions around all that, and you will be on the right path to a good life. By creating meaning and setting life goals, you give yourself direction. Make sure it is the right direction and that you avoid drift. Grab your life now and take responsibility: you will never regret doing so and your future will be yours forever.

How to design and set your personal contract

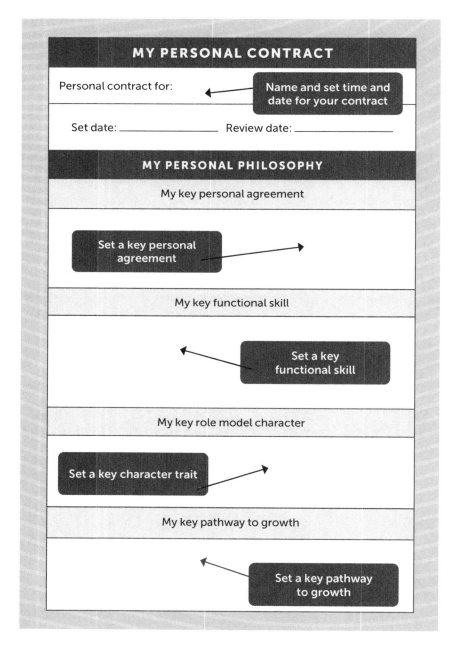

MY PERSONAL CONTRACT

Personal contract for: _____ ← Name and set time and date for your contract

Set date: _____ Review date: _____

MY PERSONAL PHILOSOPHY

My key personal agreement

Set a key personal agreement →

My key functional skill

← Set a key functional skill

My key role model character

Set a key character trait →

My key pathway to growth

← Set a key pathway to growth

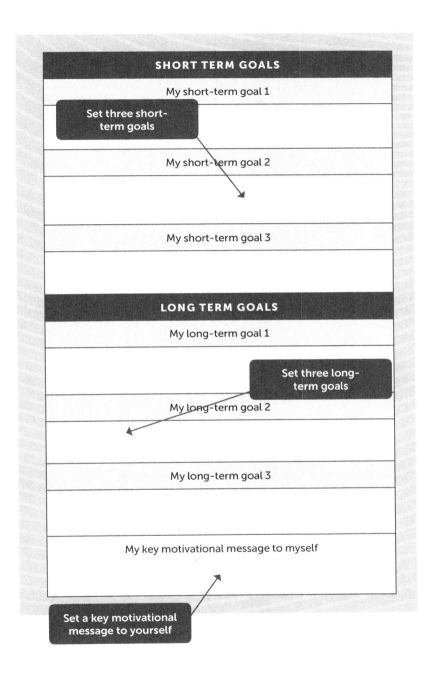

Here is an example to help you

MY PERSONAL CONTRACT

Personal contract for: **Dave Armstrong**

Set date: **4 July 2024**   Review date: **4 January 2025**

MY PERSONAL PHILOSOPHY

My key personal agreement

To be considered thoughtful and motivated, but true to my word

My key functional skill

I will improve my emotional control and reduce my impulsiveness

My key role model character

I will show leadership and courage to be who I want to be

My key pathway to growth

Always learning and listening. Never stop

SHORT TERM GOALS
My short-term goal 1
Lose weight to 12.5 stone by December 2024
My short-term goal 2
Have my 1st fiction book to the editor by end of July 2025
My short-term goal 3
Complete and consolidate this Live Life smarter programme by September 2024

LONG TERM GOALS
My long-term goal 1
To help as many people as I can to have a life they want before I die
My long-term goal 2
To become a recognised author
My long-term goal 3
To end my days happy and content with what I have done
My key motivational message to myself
Remove anger and believe everything is possible

How to write your *7 Rules to a Good Life* daily Journal

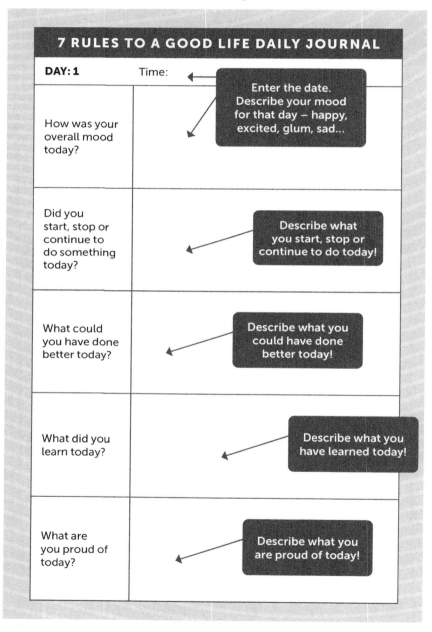

7 RULES TO A GOOD LIFE DAILY JOURNAL

DAY: 1	Time:
How was your overall mood today?	Enter the date. Describe your mood for that day – happy, excited, glum, sad...
Did you start, stop or continue to do something today?	Describe what you start, stop or continue to do today!
What could you have done better today?	Describe what you could have done better today!
What did you learn today?	Describe what you have learned today!
What are you proud of today?	Describe what you are proud of today!

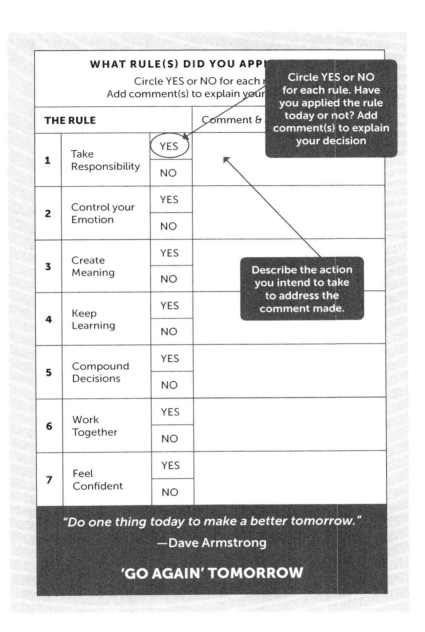

THE RULE		Comment & ...
1 Take Responsibility	YES	
	NO	
2 Control your Emotion	YES	
	NO	
3 Create Meaning	YES	
	NO	
4 Keep Learning	YES	
	NO	
5 Compound Decisions	YES	
	NO	
6 Work Together	YES	
	NO	
7 Feel Confident	YES	
	NO	

WHAT RULE(S) DID YOU APPL[Y]
Circle YES or NO for each r...
Add comment(s) to explain you...

Circle YES or NO for each rule. Have you applied the rule today or not? Add comment(s) to explain your decision

Describe the action you intend to take to address the comment made.

"Do one thing today to make a better tomorrow."
—Dave Armstrong

'GO AGAIN' TOMORROW

How to write your weekly reflection
– Did you drift or gain this week?

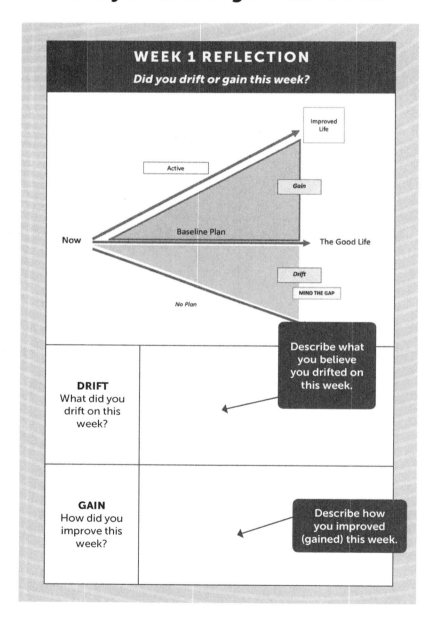

How to write your weekly Good Life Challenges

Set your challenges from either your Wheel of a Balanced Life or your Peak Performance Profile.

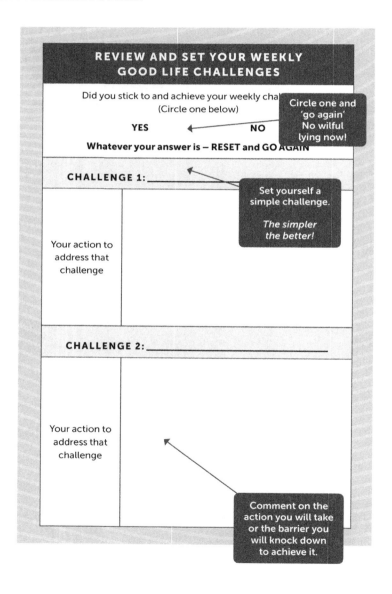

NOTES

How to set your
Wheel of a Balanced Life

FOR THIS EXERCISE, look at one of the 12 principles of the Wheel of a Balanced Life in isolation and mark yourself with a score from one to ten. Ten is the highest score you can give yourself: meaning you are currently very happy and fulfilled, working at your best within that area. A score of one indicates you are very unhappy and have lost yourself within that area. If you mark one in any area, you must investigate it as a matter of urgency and reflect on how you will improve that score.

So, scale your feelings from one to ten. The key point here is you must be honest with yourself. No wilful lying or pretending that your reality is different. Control your emotions around what you are thinking and mark it in the moment you assess that area. By doing this, you can create and consolidate an authentic plan and solution for improving a poor score or maintaining a high score. You will give each element clear direction by the creation of meaning within each area. The aim is to make your life safer and happier. From this will come more security and more success in life.

How to improve your scores

Now reflect upon your scores and create solutions for improvement in all the areas that need it. Once you have been through all the areas, you will have a series of scores from one to ten. Doing this exercise, you will receive your own agency moments. Study the information you see across the lines you have created, and you will start feeling the agency within your mind. Don't forget to control your emotions (Rule 2) by ensuring what you rely on mentally is authentic and honest; and create meaning (Rule 3) by giving yourself direction with an achievable goal for each area. You can now make choices and take agency in each area regarding what actions, in which order, you want to put in place to address each one; especially if you have some low scores. Look at your low scores. Identify those areas that you need to focus on. Then create a plan to address the lower scores and work towards making them a score of ten. Remember: you are where you are, so keep learning, set focussed personal challenges, build on good habits and develop new behaviours. Enjoy what you do and be positive in your future direction. The power is now with you.

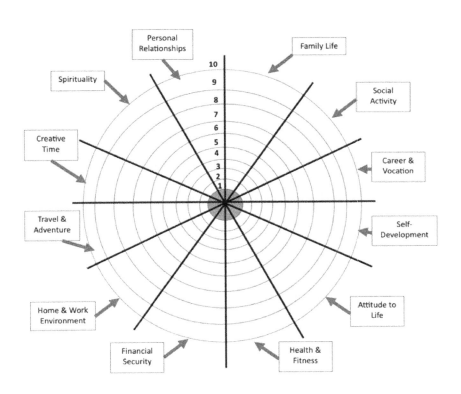

How to approach your Peak Performance Profile exercise

THESE TWELVE LIFE PRINCIPLES that drive Peak Performance give you some headings to work on to achieve a good life. This is an exercise you can use at any time, by assessing on a scale of one to ten how good or bad you are in each area, one being the lowest and ten meaning you excel in that area. So, look at each of the twelve areas and think how it applies to you now. As with the Wheel of a Balanced Life exercise earlier, scale your feelings from one to ten. The key point once again is you must be honest with yourself: no wilful lying or pretending that your reality is different. So, control your emotion around what you are thinking as you assess and mark each area.

As you did with the Wheel of a Balanced Life, reflect upon the marks and create solutions for improvement in all areas that need it. Once you have worked through all the principles, you will have a series of scores from one to ten. By doing the exercise you have given yourself agency. With the information you absorb, you will start feeling that agency. Do not forget to control your emotions and create meaning for each area. You can now make choices and take agency by deciding which actions in what order you put in place; especially if you have some low scores. Identify those areas that you need to focus on. Then create a plan to address the lower score and work towards a score of ten.

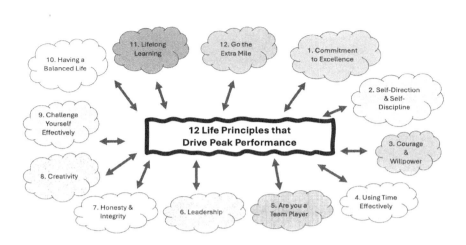

Remember: you are where you are, so keep learning to develop and strengthen new habits. Enjoy what you do and be positive in your future direction.

How to write and log your experiences

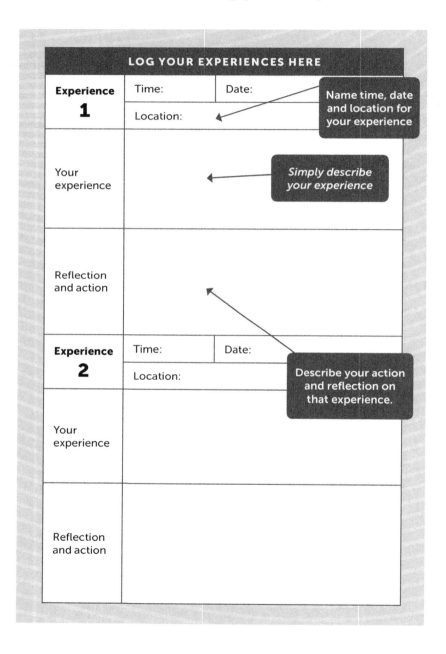

NOTES

JOURNAL STARTS HERE!

NAME

_____

START DATE

_____

SIGNATURE

_____

PART 1:
Journal Set-Up

This part forms the foundation of your journal.

Now carry out the following exercises prior to the commencement of your *7 Rules to a Good Life 28-Day Journal*.

1. Set your Personal Contract

2. Design your Wheel of a Balanced Life

3. Design your Peak Performance Profile

4. Set your 28-Day Good Life Challenges

MY PERSONAL CONTRACT

Personal contract for:

Set date: _____ Review date: _____

MY PERSONAL PHILOSOPHY

My key personal agreement

My key functional skill

My key role model character

My key pathway to growth

SHORT TERM GOALS

My short-term goal 1

My short-term goal 2

My short-term goal 3

LONG TERM GOALS

My long-term goal 1

My long-term goal 2

My long-term goal 3

My key motivational message to myself

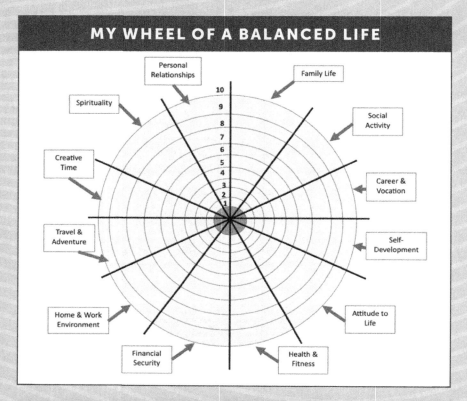

MY WHEEL OF A BALANCED LIFE

	SCORE	COMMENTS/ACTIONS
Family Life		
Social Activity		
Career & Vocation		
Self-Development		
Attitude to Life		

Health & Fitness		
Financial Security		
Home & Work Environment		
Travel & Adventure		
Creative Time		
Spirituality		
Personal Relationships		

....

....

....

....

....

....

NOTES

MY PEAK PERFORMANCE PROFILE

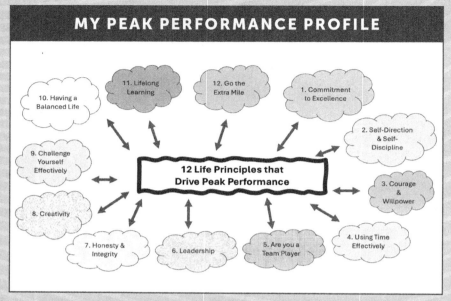

	SCORE	COMMENTS/ACTIONS
Commitment to Excellence		
Self-Direction & Self-Discipline		
Courage and Willpower		
Using Time Effectively		
Are you a Team Player?		

Leadership		
Honesty & Integrity		
Creativity		
Challenge Yourself Effectively		
Having a Balanced Life		
Life-long Learning		
Go the Extra Mile		

....
....
....
....
....
....
....

NOTES

MY 28-DAY GOOD LIFE CHALLENGES

Set your challenges to drive your goals from either your Wheel of a Balanced Life or your Peak Performance Profile.

CHALLENGE 1: _____

Your action to address that challenge	

CHALLENGE 2: _____

Your action to address that challenge	

CHALLENGE 3: _____

Your action to address that challenge	

CHALLENGE 4: _____

Your action to address that challenge	

PART 2:

Now drive and direct your personal development plan journal

What you do now, writing on a daily basis, forms the substance of your Journal and sets your future learning habits and outstanding behaviours.

Remember to open your 'Gateway to Learning'.

And once you do...
keep it open.

7 RULES TO A GOOD LIFE DAILY JOURNAL

DAY: 1	Time:	Date:
How was your overall mood today?		
Did you start, stop or continue to do something today?		
What could you have done better today?		
What did you learn today?		
What are you proud of today?		

WHAT RULE(S) DID YOU APPLY TODAY?

Circle YES or NO for each rule.
Add comment(s) to explain your decision.

THE RULE			Comment & action for tomorrow
1	Take Responsibility	YES	
		NO	
2	Control your Emotion	YES	
		NO	
3	Create Meaning	YES	
		NO	
4	Keep Learning	YES	
		NO	
5	Compound Decisions	YES	
		NO	
6	Work Together	YES	
		NO	
7	Feel Confident	YES	
		NO	

"Do one thing today to make a better tomorrow."
—Dave Armstrong

'GO AGAIN' TOMORROW

7 RULES TO A GOOD LIFE DAILY JOURNAL

DAY: 2   Time: Date:

How was your overall mood today?	
Did you start, stop or continue to do something today?	
What could you have done better today?	
What did you learn today?	
What are you proud of today?	

WHAT RULE(S) DID YOU APPLY TODAY?

Circle YES or NO for each rule.
Add comment(s) to explain your decision.

THE RULE			Comment & action for tomorrow
1	Take Responsibility	YES	
		NO	
2	Control your Emotion	YES	
		NO	
3	Create Meaning	YES	
		NO	
4	Keep Learning	YES	
		NO	
5	Compound Decisions	YES	
		NO	
6	Work Together	YES	
		NO	
7	Feel Confident	YES	
		NO	

"It's never too late to be what you might have been."
—George Eliot

'GO AGAIN' TOMORROW

7 RULES TO A GOOD LIFE DAILY JOURNAL

DAY: 3	Time:	Date:
How was your overall mood today?		
Did you start, stop or continue to do something today?		
What could you have done better today?		
What did you learn today?		
What are you proud of today?		

WHAT RULE(S) DID YOU APPLY TODAY?

Circle YES or NO for each rule.
Add comment(s) to explain your decision.

THE RULE			Comment & action for tomorrow
1	Take Responsibility	YES	
		NO	
2	Control your Emotion	YES	
		NO	
3	Create Meaning	YES	
		NO	
4	Keep Learning	YES	
		NO	
5	Compound Decisions	YES	
		NO	
6	Work Together	YES	
		NO	
7	Feel Confident	YES	
		NO	

"The happiness of your life depends upon the quality of your thoughts." —Marcus Aurelius

'GO AGAIN' TOMORROW

7 RULES TO A GOOD LIFE DAILY JOURNAL

DAY: 4 Time: Date:

How was your overall mood today?	
Did you start, stop or continue to do something today?	
What could you have done better today?	
What did you learn today?	
What are you proud of today?	

WHAT RULE(S) DID YOU APPLY TODAY?

Circle YES or NO for each rule.
Add comment(s) to explain your decision.

THE RULE			Comment & action for tomorrow
1	Take Responsibility	YES	
		NO	
2	Control your Emotion	YES	
		NO	
3	Create Meaning	YES	
		NO	
4	Keep Learning	YES	
		NO	
5	Compound Decisions	YES	
		NO	
6	Work Together	YES	
		NO	
7	Feel Confident	YES	
		NO	

"We are what we repeatedly do. Excellence then is a habit." —Socrates

'GO AGAIN' TOMORROW

7 RULES TO A GOOD LIFE DAILY JOURNAL

DAY: 5   Time: Date:

How was your overall mood today?	
Did you start, stop or continue to do something today?	
What could you have done better today?	
What did you learn today?	
What are you proud of today?	

WHAT RULE(S) DID YOU APPLY TODAY?

Circle YES or NO for each rule.
Add comment(s) to explain your decision.

THE RULE			Comment & action for tomorrow
1	Take Responsibility	YES	
		NO	
2	Control your Emotion	YES	
		NO	
3	Create Meaning	YES	
		NO	
4	Keep Learning	YES	
		NO	
5	Compound Decisions	YES	
		NO	
6	Work Together	YES	
		NO	
7	Feel Confident	YES	
		NO	

"The first and the best victory is to conquer self."
—Plato

'GO AGAIN' TOMORROW

7 RULES TO A GOOD LIFE DAILY JOURNAL

DAY: 6   Time: Date:

How was your overall mood today?	
Did you start, stop or continue to do something today?	
What could you have done better today?	
What did you learn today?	
What are you proud of today?	

WHAT RULE(S) DID YOU APPLY TODAY?

Circle YES or NO for each rule.
Add comment(s) to explain your decision.

THE RULE			Comment & action for tomorrow
1	Take Responsibility	YES	
		NO	
2	Control your Emotion	YES	
		NO	
3	Create Meaning	YES	
		NO	
4	Keep Learning	YES	
		NO	
5	Compound Decisions	YES	
		NO	
6	Work Together	YES	
		NO	
7	Feel Confident	YES	
		NO	

"It's not what happens to you, but how you react to it that matters." —Epictetus

'GO AGAIN' TOMORROW

7 RULES TO A GOOD LIFE DAILY JOURNAL

DAY: 7   Time: Date:

How was your overall mood today?	
Did you start, stop or continue to do something today?	
What could you have done better today?	
What did you learn today?	
What are you proud of today?	

WHAT RULE(S) DID YOU APPLY TODAY?

Circle YES or NO for each rule.
Add comment(s) to explain your decision.

THE RULE			Comment & action for tomorrow
1	Take Responsibility	YES	
		NO	
2	Control your Emotion	YES	
		NO	
3	Create Meaning	YES	
		NO	
4	Keep Learning	YES	
		NO	
5	Compound Decisions	YES	
		NO	
6	Work Together	YES	
		NO	
7	Feel Confident	YES	
		NO	

"Failure is success in progress."
—Albert Einstein

'GO AGAIN' TOMORROW

WEEK 1 REFLECTION
Did you drift or gain this week?

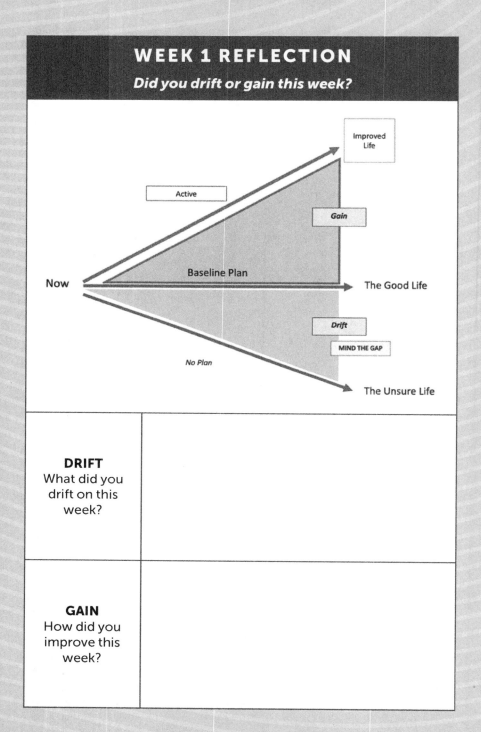

DRIFT What did you drift on this week?	
GAIN How did you improve this week?	

What will you do this week to prevent drift
and drive your Good Life gain?

REVIEW AND SET YOUR WEEKLY GOOD LIFE CHALLENGES

Did you stick to and achieve your weekly challenges?
(Circle one below)

YES   **NO**

Whatever your answer is — RESET and GO AGAIN

CHALLENGE 1: _____

Your action to address that challenge	

CHALLENGE 2: _____

Your action to address that challenge	

CHALLENGE 3: _____

Your action to
address that
challenge

CHALLENGE 4: _____

Your action to
address that
challenge

7 RULES TO A GOOD LIFE DAILY JOURNAL

DAY: 8   Time: Date:

How was your overall mood today?	
Did you start, stop or continue to do something today?	
What could you have done better today?	
What did you learn today?	
What are you proud of today?	

WHAT RULE(S) DID YOU APPLY TODAY?

Circle YES or NO for each rule.
Add comment(s) to explain your decision.

THE RULE			Comment & action for tomorrow
1	Take Responsibility	YES	
		NO	
2	Control your Emotion	YES	
		NO	
3	Create Meaning	YES	
		NO	
4	Keep Learning	YES	
		NO	
5	Compound Decisions	YES	
		NO	
6	Work Together	YES	
		NO	
7	Feel Confident	YES	
		NO	

"Enjoy life. This is not a dress rehearsal."
—Friedrich Nietzsche

'GO AGAIN' TOMORROW

7 RULES TO A GOOD LIFE DAILY JOURNAL

DAY: 9	Time:	Date:

How was your overall mood today?	

Did you start, stop or continue to do something today?	

What could you have done better today?	

What did you learn today?	

What are you proud of today?	

WHAT RULE(S) DID YOU APPLY TODAY?

Circle YES or NO for each rule.
Add comment(s) to explain your decision.

THE RULE			Comment & action for tomorrow
1	Take Responsibility	YES	
		NO	
2	Control your Emotion	YES	
		NO	
3	Create Meaning	YES	
		NO	
4	Keep Learning	YES	
		NO	
5	Compound Decisions	YES	
		NO	
6	Work Together	YES	
		NO	
7	Feel Confident	YES	
		NO	

"Our greatest freedom is the freedom to choose our attitude." —Viktor E. Frankl

'GO AGAIN' TOMORROW

7 RULES TO A GOOD LIFE DAILY JOURNAL

DAY: 10 Time: Date:

How was your overall mood today?	
Did you start, stop or continue to do something today?	
What could you have done better today?	
What did you learn today?	
What are you proud of today?	

WHAT RULE(S) DID YOU APPLY TODAY?
Circle YES or NO for each rule.
Add comment(s) to explain your decision.

THE RULE			Comment & action for tomorrow
1	Take Responsibility	YES	
		NO	
2	Control your Emotion	YES	
		NO	
3	Create Meaning	YES	
		NO	
4	Keep Learning	YES	
		NO	
5	Compound Decisions	YES	
		NO	
6	Work Together	YES	
		NO	
7	Feel Confident	YES	
		NO	

"All good thoughts and ideas mean nothing without action." —Mahatma Gandhi

'GO AGAIN' TOMORROW

7 RULES TO A GOOD LIFE DAILY JOURNAL

DAY: 11   Time: Date:

How was your overall mood today?	
Did you start, stop or continue to do something today?	
What could you have done better today?	
What did you learn today?	
What are you proud of today?	

WHAT RULE(S) DID YOU APPLY TODAY?

Circle YES or NO for each rule.
Add comment(s) to explain your decision.

THE RULE			Comment & action for tomorrow
1	Take Responsibility	YES	
		NO	
2	Control your Emotion	YES	
		NO	
3	Create Meaning	YES	
		NO	
4	Keep Learning	YES	
		NO	
5	Compound Decisions	YES	
		NO	
6	Work Together	YES	
		NO	
7	Feel Confident	YES	
		NO	

"You cannot escape the responsibility of tomorrow by evading it today." —Abraham Lincoln

'GO AGAIN' TOMORROW

7 RULES TO A GOOD LIFE DAILY JOURNAL

DAY: 12	Time:	Date:
How was your overall mood today?		
Did you start, stop or continue to do something today?		
What could you have done better today?		
What did you learn today?		
What are you proud of today?		

WHAT RULE(S) DID YOU APPLY TODAY?

Circle YES or NO for each rule.
Add comment(s) to explain your decision.

THE RULE			Comment & action for tomorrow
1	Take Responsibility	YES	
		NO	
2	Control your Emotion	YES	
		NO	
3	Create Meaning	YES	
		NO	
4	Keep Learning	YES	
		NO	
5	Compound Decisions	YES	
		NO	
6	Work Together	YES	
		NO	
7	Feel Confident	YES	
		NO	

"If you learn from defeat, you haven't really lost."
—Zig Ziglar

'GO AGAIN' TOMORROW

7 RULES TO A GOOD LIFE DAILY JOURNAL

DAY: 13   Time: Date:

How was your overall mood today?	
Did you start, stop or continue to do something today?	
What could you have done better today?	
What did you learn today?	
What are you proud of today?	

WHAT RULE(S) DID YOU APPLY TODAY? Circle YES or NO for each rule. Add comment(s) to explain your decision.		
THE RULE		Comment & action for tomorrow
1 Take Responsibility	YES	
	NO	
2 Control your Emotion	YES	
	NO	
3 Create Meaning	YES	
	NO	
4 Keep Learning	YES	
	NO	
5 Compound Decisions	YES	
	NO	
6 Work Together	YES	
	NO	
7 Feel Confident	YES	
	NO	

"Your life does not get better by chance; it gets better by change." —Jim Rohn

'GO AGAIN' TOMORROW

7 RULES TO A GOOD LIFE DAILY JOURNAL

DAY: 14	Time:	Date:
How was your overall mood today?		
Did you start, stop or continue to do something today?		
What could you have done better today?		
What did you learn today?		
What are you proud of today?		

WHAT RULE(S) DID YOU APPLY TODAY?
Circle YES or NO for each rule.
Add comment(s) to explain your decision.

THE RULE			Comment & action for tomorrow
1	Take Responsibility	YES	
		NO	
2	Control your Emotion	YES	
		NO	
3	Create Meaning	YES	
		NO	
4	Keep Learning	YES	
		NO	
5	Compound Decisions	YES	
		NO	
6	Work Together	YES	
		NO	
7	Feel Confident	YES	
		NO	

"Work as hard as you possibly can on at least one thing and see what happens." —Jordan Peterson

'GO AGAIN' TOMORROW

WEEK 2 REFLECTION
Did you drift or gain this week?

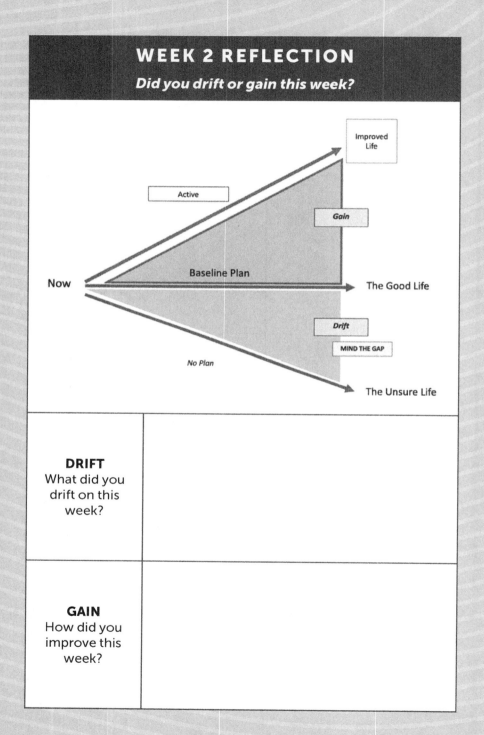

DRIFT What did you drift on this week?	
GAIN How did you improve this week?	

What will you do this week to prevent drift
and drive your Good Life gain?

REVIEW AND SET YOUR WEEKLY GOOD LIFE CHALLENGES

Did you stick to and achieve your weekly challenges?
(Circle one below)

YES   **NO**

Whatever your answer is — RESET and GO AGAIN

CHALLENGE 1: _____

Your action to address that challenge	

CHALLENGE 2: _____

Your action to address that challenge	

CHALLENGE 3: _____

Your action to address that challenge

CHALLENGE 4: _____

Your action to address that challenge

7 RULES TO A GOOD LIFE DAILY JOURNAL

DAY: 15 Time: Date:

How was your overall mood today?	
Did you start, stop or continue to do something today?	
What could you have done better today?	
What did you learn today?	
What are you proud of today?	

WHAT RULE(S) DID YOU APPLY TODAY?
Circle YES or NO for each rule.
Add comment(s) to explain your decision.

THE RULE			Comment & action for tomorrow
1	Take Responsibility	YES	
		NO	
2	Control your Emotion	YES	
		NO	
3	Create Meaning	YES	
		NO	
4	Keep Learning	YES	
		NO	
5	Compound Decisions	YES	
		NO	
6	Work Together	YES	
		NO	
7	Feel Confident	YES	
		NO	

"Age is no barrier. It is the limitation you put on your mind." —Jackie Joyner-Kersee

'GO AGAIN' TOMORROW

7 RULES TO A GOOD LIFE DAILY JOURNAL

DAY: 16   Time: Date:

How was your overall mood today?	
Did you start, stop or continue to do something today?	
What could you have done better today?	
What did you learn today?	
What are you proud of today?	

WHAT RULE(S) DID YOU APPLY TODAY?

Circle YES or NO for each rule.
Add comment(s) to explain your decision.

THE RULE			Comment & action for tomorrow
1	Take Responsibility	YES	
		NO	
2	Control your Emotion	YES	
		NO	
3	Create Meaning	YES	
		NO	
4	Keep Learning	YES	
		NO	
5	Compound Decisions	YES	
		NO	
6	Work Together	YES	
		NO	
7	Feel Confident	YES	
		NO	

"Choose to be optimistic; it feels better."

—Dali Lama

'GO AGAIN' TOMORROW

7 RULES TO A GOOD LIFE DAILY JOURNAL

DAY: 17　　　Time:　　　　　　Date:

How was your overall mood today?	
Did you start, stop or continue to do something today?	
What could you have done better today?	
What did you learn today?	
What are you proud of today?	

WHAT RULE(S) DID YOU APPLY TODAY?

Circle YES or NO for each rule.
Add comment(s) to explain your decision.

THE RULE			Comment & action for tomorrow
1	Take Responsibility	YES	
		NO	
2	Control your Emotion	YES	
		NO	
3	Create Meaning	YES	
		NO	
4	Keep Learning	YES	
		NO	
5	Compound Decisions	YES	
		NO	
6	Work Together	YES	
		NO	
7	Feel Confident	YES	
		NO	

"You can, you should and, if you're brave enough to start, you will." —Stephen King

'GO AGAIN' TOMORROW

7 RULES TO A GOOD LIFE DAILY JOURNAL

DAY: 18   Time: Date:

How was your overall mood today?	
Did you start, stop or continue to do something today?	
What could you have done better today?	
What did you learn today?	
What are you proud of today?	

WHAT RULE(S) DID YOU APPLY TODAY?

Circle YES or NO for each rule.
Add comment(s) to explain your decision.

THE RULE			Comment & action for tomorrow
1	Take Responsibility	YES	
		NO	
2	Control your Emotion	YES	
		NO	
3	Create Meaning	YES	
		NO	
4	Keep Learning	YES	
		NO	
5	Compound Decisions	YES	
		NO	
6	Work Together	YES	
		NO	
7	Feel Confident	YES	
		NO	

"You cannot change what you are, only what you do." —Phillip Pullman

'GO AGAIN' TOMORROW

7 RULES TO A GOOD LIFE DAILY JOURNAL

DAY: 19   Time: Date:

How was your overall mood today?	
Did you start, stop or continue to do something today?	
What could you have done better today?	
What did you learn today?	
What are you proud of today?	

WHAT RULE(S) DID YOU APPLY TODAY?

Circle YES or NO for each rule.
Add comment(s) to explain your decision.

THE RULE			Comment & action for tomorrow
1	Take Responsibility	YES	
		NO	
2	Control your Emotion	YES	
		NO	
3	Create Meaning	YES	
		NO	
4	Keep Learning	YES	
		NO	
5	Compound Decisions	YES	
		NO	
6	Work Together	YES	
		NO	
7	Feel Confident	YES	
		NO	

"If you see someone without a smile, give them yours."
—Dolly Parton

'GO AGAIN' TOMORROW

7 RULES TO A GOOD LIFE DAILY JOURNAL

DAY: 20   Time: Date:

How was your overall mood today?	
Did you start, stop or continue to do something today?	
What could you have done better today?	
What did you learn today?	
What are you proud of today?	

WHAT RULE(S) DID YOU APPLY TODAY?

Circle YES or NO for each rule.
Add comment(s) to explain your decision.

THE RULE			Comment & action for tomorrow
1	Take Responsibility	YES	
		NO	
2	Control your Emotion	YES	
		NO	
3	Create Meaning	YES	
		NO	
4	Keep Learning	YES	
		NO	
5	Compound Decisions	YES	
		NO	
6	Work Together	YES	
		NO	
7	Feel Confident	YES	
		NO	

"The secret of getting ahead is getting started."
—Mark Twain

'GO AGAIN' TOMORROW

7 RULES TO A GOOD LIFE DAILY JOURNAL

DAY: 21	Time:	Date:
How was your overall mood today?		
Did you start, stop or continue to do something today?		
What could you have done better today?		
What did you learn today?		
What are you proud of today?		

WHAT RULE(S) DID YOU APPLY TODAY?

Circle YES or NO for each rule.
Add comment(s) to explain your decision.

THE RULE			Comment & action for tomorrow
1	Take Responsibility	YES	
		NO	
2	Control your Emotion	YES	
		NO	
3	Create Meaning	YES	
		NO	
4	Keep Learning	YES	
		NO	
5	Compound Decisions	YES	
		NO	
6	Work Together	YES	
		NO	
7	Feel Confident	YES	
		NO	

"You don't have to see the whole staircase, just take the first step." —Martin Luther King Jr.

'GO AGAIN' TOMORROW

WEEK 3 REFLECTION
Did you drift or gain this week?

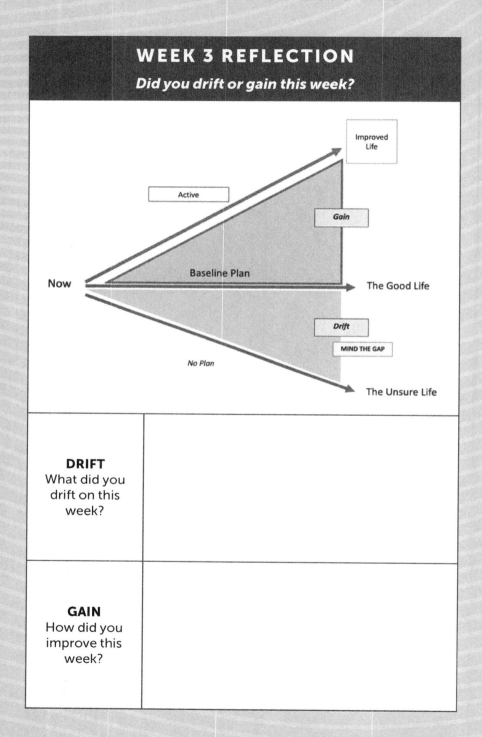

DRIFT What did you drift on this week?	
GAIN How did you improve this week?	

**What will you do this week to prevent drift
and drive your Good Life gain?**

REVIEW AND SET YOUR WEEKLY GOOD LIFE CHALLENGES

Did you stick to and achieve your weekly challenges?
(Circle one below)

YES   **NO**

Whatever your answer is — RESET and GO AGAIN

CHALLENGE 1: _____

Your action to address that challenge	

CHALLENGE 2: _____

Your action to address that challenge	

CHALLENGE 3: _____

Your action to address that challenge	

CHALLENGE 4: _____

Your action to address that challenge	

7 RULES TO A GOOD LIFE DAILY JOURNAL

DAY: 22	Time:	Date:
How was your overall mood today?		
Did you start, stop or continue to do something today?		
What could you have done better today?		
What did you learn today?		
What are you proud of today?		

WHAT RULE(S) DID YOU APPLY TODAY?

Circle YES or NO for each rule.
Add comment(s) to explain your decision.

THE RULE			Comment & action for tomorrow
1	Take Responsibility	YES	
		NO	
2	Control your Emotion	YES	
		NO	
3	Create Meaning	YES	
		NO	
4	Keep Learning	YES	
		NO	
5	Compound Decisions	YES	
		NO	
6	Work Together	YES	
		NO	
7	Feel Confident	YES	
		NO	

"The more difficult the victory, the greater the happiness in winning." —Pelé

'GO AGAIN' TOMORROW

7 RULES TO A GOOD LIFE DAILY JOURNAL

DAY: 23   Time: Date:

How was your overall mood today?	
Did you start, stop or continue to do something today?	
What could you have done better today?	
What did you learn today?	
What are you proud of today?	

WHAT RULE(S) DID YOU APPLY TODAY?

Circle YES or NO for each rule.
Add comment(s) to explain your decision.

THE RULE			Comment & action for tomorrow
1	Take Responsibility	YES	
		NO	
2	Control your Emotion	YES	
		NO	
3	Create Meaning	YES	
		NO	
4	Keep Learning	YES	
		NO	
5	Compound Decisions	YES	
		NO	
6	Work Together	YES	
		NO	
7	Feel Confident	YES	
		NO	

"Some people want it to happen, some wish it would happen, others make it happen." —Michael Jordan

'GO AGAIN' TOMORROW

7 RULES TO A GOOD LIFE DAILY JOURNAL

DAY: 24	Time:	Date:
How was your overall mood today?		
Did you start, stop or continue to do something today?		
What could you have done better today?		
What did you learn today?		
What are you proud of today?		

WHAT RULE(S) DID YOU APPLY TODAY?

Circle YES or NO for each rule.
Add comment(s) to explain your decision.

THE RULE			Comment & action for tomorrow
1	Take Responsibility	YES	
		NO	
2	Control your Emotion	YES	
		NO	
3	Create Meaning	YES	
		NO	
4	Keep Learning	YES	
		NO	
5	Compound Decisions	YES	
		NO	
6	Work Together	YES	
		NO	
7	Feel Confident	YES	
		NO	

"With self-discipline, most anything is possible."
—Theodore Roosevelt

'GO AGAIN' TOMORROW

7 RULES TO A GOOD LIFE DAILY JOURNAL

DAY: 25	Time:	Date:
How was your overall mood today?		
Did you start, stop or continue to do something today?		
What could you have done better today?		
What did you learn today?		
What are you proud of today?		

WHAT RULE(S) DID YOU APPLY TODAY?

Circle YES or NO for each rule.
Add comment(s) to explain your decision.

THE RULE			Comment & action for tomorrow
1	Take Responsibility	YES	
		NO	
2	Control your Emotion	YES	
		NO	
3	Create Meaning	YES	
		NO	
4	Keep Learning	YES	
		NO	
5	Compound Decisions	YES	
		NO	
6	Work Together	YES	
		NO	
7	Feel Confident	YES	
		NO	

"I never dreamed about success. I worked for it."
—Estée Lauder

'GO AGAIN' TOMORROW

7 RULES TO A GOOD LIFE DAILY JOURNAL

DAY: 26   Time: Date:

How was your overall mood today?	
Did you start, stop or continue to do something today?	
What could you have done better today?	
What did you learn today?	
What are you proud of today?	

WHAT RULE(S) DID YOU APPLY TODAY?

Circle YES or NO for each rule.
Add comment(s) to explain your decision.

	THE RULE		Comment & action for tomorrow
1	Take Responsibility	YES	
		NO	
2	Control your Emotion	YES	
		NO	
3	Create Meaning	YES	
		NO	
4	Keep Learning	YES	
		NO	
5	Compound Decisions	YES	
		NO	
6	Work Together	YES	
		NO	
7	Feel Confident	YES	
		NO	

"In the midst of chaos, there is also opportunity."
—Sun-Tzu

'GO AGAIN' TOMORROW

7 RULES TO A GOOD LIFE DAILY JOURNAL

DAY: 27	Time:	Date:

How was your overall mood today?	
Did you start, stop or continue to do something today?	
What could you have done better today?	
What did you learn today?	
What are you proud of today?	

WHAT RULE(S) DID YOU APPLY TODAY?
Circle YES or NO for each rule.
Add comment(s) to explain your decision.

THE RULE			Comment & action for tomorrow
1	Take Responsibility	YES	
		NO	
2	Control your Emotion	YES	
		NO	
3	Create Meaning	YES	
		NO	
4	Keep Learning	YES	
		NO	
5	Compound Decisions	YES	
		NO	
6	Work Together	YES	
		NO	
7	Feel Confident	YES	
		NO	

"True love is born from understanding."
—The Buddha

'GO AGAIN' TOMORROW

7 RULES TO A GOOD LIFE DAILY JOURNAL

DAY: 28	Time:	Date:
How was your overall mood today?		
Did you start, stop or continue to do something today?		
What could you have done better today?		
What did you learn today?		
What are you proud of today?		

WHAT RULE(S) DID YOU APPLY TODAY?
Circle YES or NO for each rule.
Add comment(s) to explain your decision.

THE RULE			Comment & action for tomorrow
1	Take Responsibility	YES	
		NO	
2	Control your Emotion	YES	
		NO	
3	Create Meaning	YES	
		NO	
4	Keep Learning	YES	
		NO	
5	Compound Decisions	YES	
		NO	
6	Work Together	YES	
		NO	
7	Feel Confident	YES	
		NO	

"If you don't want to slip up tomorrow, speak the truth today." —Bruce Lee

'GO AGAIN' TOMORROW

WEEK 4 REFLECTION

Did you drift or gain this week?

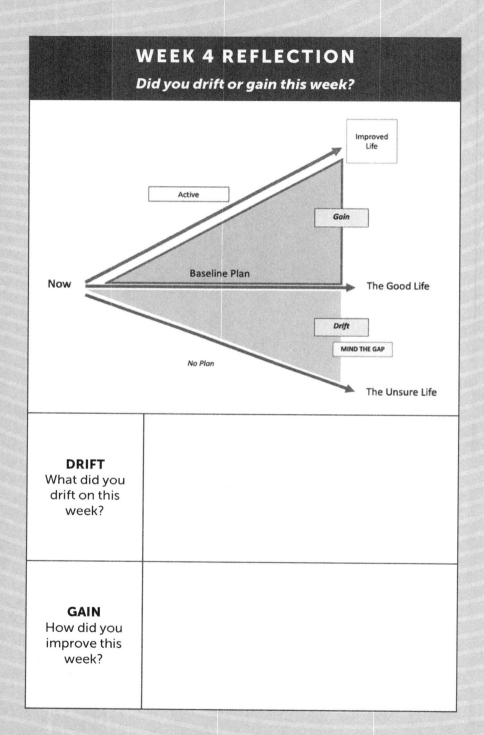

DRIFT What did you drift on this week?	
GAIN How did you improve this week?	

**What will you do this week to prevent drift
and drive your Good Life gain?**

7 RULES TO A GOOD LIFE 28-DAY JOURNAL CLOSING THOUGHTS!

How was your overall mood during the past 28 days?

Did you start, stop, or continue to do something in the past 28 days?

What could you have done better over the past 28 days?

What are you proud of over the past 28 days?

"Remember: failure does not exist. Recognise it as a moment in time to 'GO AGAIN'" —Dave Armstrong

'GO AGAIN' TOMORROW

ANY FINAL THOUGHTS BEFORE YOU CLOSE YOUR JOURNAL?

PART 3:
Close your 28-Day Personal Development Planning Journal

Well done, and be proud of what you have achieved over only 28 days.

Now you can choose to live to your Journal, or reset it for another 28 days and 'go again' tomorrow with a new 28-day Journal development period. Don't waste this opportunity and the good feelings you are now experiencing: keep on building, keep on growing and keep enjoying your life today to make a better tomorrow.

BUILD UPON this foundation you have set yourself and **GO AGAIN** by:

1. Reviewing and reflecting on your Personal Contract. Reset it, or reinforce it within your daily life.

2. Periodically reviewing and reflecting on your Wheel of a Balanced Life. (Reinforce or reset the wheel as and when required.)

3. Periodically reviewing and reflecting on your Peak Performance Profile. (Reinforce or reset the profile as and when required.)

4. Developing your 28-Day Good Life Challenges into Life Goal Challenges.

WRITE YOUR RENEWED PERSONAL CONTRACT

Personal contract for:

Set date: _____ Review date: _____

MY PERSONAL PHILOSOPHY

My key personal agreement

My key functional skill

My key role model character

My key pathway to growth

SHORT TERM GOALS

My short-term goal 1

My short-term goal 2

My short-term goal 3

LONG TERM GOALS

My long-term goal 1

My long-term goal 2

My long-term goal 3

My key motivational message to myself

NOTES

MY REFLECTIONS AT THE END OF 28 DAYS
WHEEL OF A BALANCED LIFE

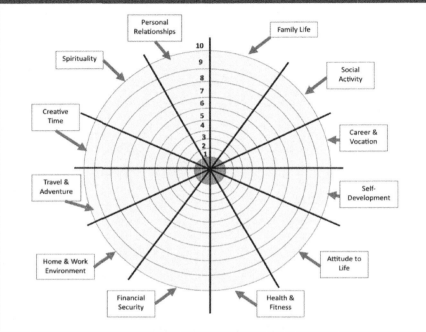

	SCORE	COMMENTS/ACTIONS
Family Life		
Social Activity		
Career & Vocation		
Self-Development		
Attitude to Life		

Health & Fitness		
Financial Security		
Home & Work Environment		
Travel & Adventure		
Creative Time		
Spirituality		
Personal Relationships		

....
....
....
....
....
....

MY WHEEL OF A BALANCED LIFE
FINAL THOUGHTS

MY REFLECTIONS AT THE END OF 28 DAYS
PEAK PERFORMANCE PROFILE

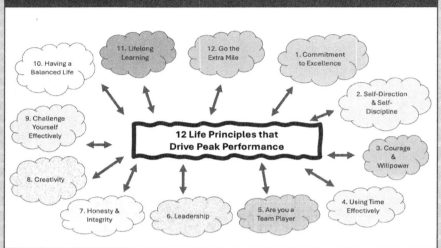

	SCORE	COMMENTS/ACTIONS
Commitment to Excellence		
Self-Direction & Self-Discipline		
Courage and Willpower		
Using Time Effectively		
Are you a Team Player?		

Leadership		
Honesty & Integrity		
Creativity		
Challenge Yourself Effectively		
Having a Balanced Life		
Life-long Learning		
Go the Extra Mile		

MY PEAK PERFORMANCE PROFILE
FINAL THOUGHTS

LOG YOUR EXPERIENCES HERE		
Experience 1	Time:	Date:
	Location:	
Your experience		
Reflection and action		
Experience 2	Time:	Date:
	Location:	
Your experience		
Reflection and action		

Experience 3	Time:	Date:
	Location:	
Your experience		
Reflection and action		

Experience 4	Time:	Date:
	Location:	
Your experience		
Reflection and action		

Experience 5	Time:	Date:
	Location:	
Your experience		
Reflection and action		

Experience 6	Time:	Date:
	Location:	
Your experience		
Reflection and action		

Experience 7	Time:	Date:
	Location:	
Your experience		
Reflection and action		

NB: It is the experiences you allow yourself to receive that feeds how your life will develop.
Choose experiences wisely!

Finally, a few inspirational words from the Philosopher King:

"Everyone's life lies in the present;
for the past is spent and done with,
and the future is uncertain."

"The happiness of your life depends
upon the quality of your thoughts."

"Each day provides its own gifts."

**Marcus Aurelius —
(Roman Emperor from 161 to 180 AD)**

You only have ONE LIFE. Make sure it is a GOOD ONE!

If you feel you need some extra support or guidance to 'go again', please do not hesitate to contact me via my website (one-to-one or group meetings available,face-to-face or virtual): https://7rules2agoodlife.com

I have various offerings, from bespoke themed sessions across a full progamme of coaching modules to one-to one-personal development coaching. All support this 28-day personal development planning Journal.

NOTES